2016 SQA Past Papers & Hodder Gibson Model Papers With Answers

National 5
MATHEMATICS

Model Paper, 2014, 2015 & 2016 Exams

HODDER
GIBSON
AN HACHETTE UK COMPANY

This book contains the official SQA 2014, 2015 and 2016 Exams for National 5 Mathematics, with associated SQA-approved answers modified from the official marking instructions that accompany the paper.

In addition the book contains a model paper, together with answers, plus study skills advice. This paper, which may include a limited number of previously published SQA questions, has been specially commissioned by Hodder Gibson, and has been written by experienced senior teachers and examiners in line with the new National 5 syllabus and assessment outlines. This is not SQA material but has been devised to provide further practice for National 5 examinations.

Hodder Gibson is grateful to the copyright holders, as credited on the final page of the Answer Section, for permission to use their material. Every effort has been made to trace the copyright holders and to obtain their permission for the use of copyright material. Hodder Gibson will be happy to receive information allowing us to rectify any error or omission in future editions.

Hachette UK's policy is to use papers that are natural, renewable and recyclable products and made from wood grown in sustainable forests. The logging and manufacturing processes are expected to conform to the environmental regulations of the country of origin.

Orders: please contact Bookpoint Ltd, 130 Park Drive, Milton Park, Abingdon, Oxon OX14 4SE. Telephone: (44) 01235 827720. Fax: (44) 01235 400454. Lines are open 9.00–5.00, Monday to Saturday, with a 24-hour message answering service. Visit our website at www.hoddereducation.co.uk. Hodder Gibson can be contacted direct on: Tel: 0141 333 4650; Fax: 0141 404 8188; email: hoddergibson@hodder.co.uk

This collection first published in 2016 by
Hodder Gibson, an imprint of Hodder Education,
An Hachette UK Company
211 St Vincent Street
Glasgow G2 5QY

Typeset by Aptara, Inc.

Printed in the UK

A catalogue record for this title is available from the British Library

ISBN: 978-1-4718-9116-8

3 2 1

2017 2016

Introduction

Study Skills – what you need to know to pass exams!

Pause for thought

Many students might skip quickly through a page like this. After all, we all know how to revise. Do you really though?

Think about this:

"IF YOU ALWAYS DO WHAT YOU ALWAYS DO, YOU WILL ALWAYS GET WHAT YOU HAVE ALWAYS GOT."

Do you like the grades you get? Do you want to do better? If you get full marks in your assessment, then that's great! Change nothing! This section is just to help you get that little bit better than you already are.

There are two main parts to the advice on offer here. The first part highlights fairly obvious things but which are also very important. The second part makes suggestions about revision that you might not have thought about but which WILL help you.

Part 1

DOH! It's so obvious but …

Start revising in good time

Don't leave it until the last minute – this will make you panic.

Make a revision timetable that sets out work time AND play time.

Sleep and eat!

Obvious really, and very helpful. Avoid arguments or stressful things too – even games that wind you up. You need to be fit, awake and focused!

Know your place!

Make sure you know exactly **WHEN and WHERE** your exams are.

Know your enemy!

Make sure you know what to expect in the exam.

How is the paper structured?

How much time is there for each question?

What types of question are involved?

Which topics seem to come up time and time again?

Which topics are your strongest and which are your weakest?

Are all topics compulsory or are there choices?

Learn by DOING!

There is no substitute for past papers and practice papers – they are simply essential! Tackling this collection of papers and answers is exactly the right thing to be doing as your exams approach.

Part 2

People learn in different ways. Some like low light, some bright. Some like early morning, some like evening / night. Some prefer warm, some prefer cold. But everyone uses their BRAIN and the brain works when it is active. Passive learning – sitting gazing at notes – is the most INEFFICIENT way to learn anything. Below you will find tips and ideas for making your revision more effective and maybe even more enjoyable. What follows gets your brain active, and active learning works!

Activity 1 – Stop and review

Step 1

When you have done no more than 5 minutes of revision reading STOP!

Step 2

Write a heading in your own words which sums up the topic you have been revising.

Step 3

Write a summary of what you have revised in no more than two sentences. Don't fool yourself by saying, "I know it, but I cannot put it into words". That just means you don't know it well enough. If you cannot write your summary, revise that section again, knowing that you must write a summary at the end of it. Many of you will have notebooks full of blue/black ink writing. Many of the pages will not be especially attractive or memorable so try to liven them up a bit with colour as you are reviewing and rewriting. **This is a great memory aid, and memory is the most important thing.**

Activity 2 – Use technology!

Why should everything be written down? Have you thought about "mental" maps, diagrams, cartoons and colour to help you learn? And rather than write down notes, why not record your revision material?

What about having a text message revision session with friends? Keep in touch with them to find out how and what they are revising and share ideas and questions.

Why not make a video diary where you tell the camera what you are doing, what you think you have learned and what you still have to do? No one has to see or hear it, but the process of having to organise your thoughts in a formal way to explain something is a very important learning practice.

Be sure to make use of electronic files. You could begin to summarise your class notes. Your typing might be slow, but it will get faster and the typed notes will be easier to read than the scribbles in your class notes. Try to add different fonts and colours to make your work stand out. You can easily Google relevant pictures, cartoons and diagrams which you can copy and paste to make your work more attractive and **MEMORABLE**.

Activity 3 – This is it. Do this and you will know lots!

Step 1

In this task you must be very honest with yourself! Find the SQA syllabus for your subject (www.sqa.org.uk). Look at how it is broken down into main topics called MANDATORY knowledge. That means stuff you MUST know.

Step 2

BEFORE you do ANY revision on this topic, write a list of everything that you already know about the subject. It might be quite a long list but you only need to write it once. It shows you all the information that is already in your long-term memory so you know what parts you do not need to revise!

Step 3

Pick a chapter or section from your book or revision notes. Choose a fairly large section or a whole chapter to get the most out of this activity.

With a buddy, use Skype, Facetime, Twitter or any other communication you have, to play the game "If this is the answer, what is the question?". For example, if you are revising Geography and the answer you provide is "meander", your buddy would have to make up a question like "What is the word that describes a feature of a river where it flows slowly and bends often from side to side?".

Make up 10 "answers" based on the content of the chapter or section you are using. Give this to your buddy to solve while you solve theirs.

Step 4

Construct a wordsearch of at least 10 × 10 squares. You can make it as big as you like but keep it realistic. Work together with a group of friends. Many apps allow you to make wordsearch puzzles online. The words and phrases can go in any direction and phrases can be split. Your puzzle must only contain facts linked to the topic you are revising. Your task is to find 10 bits of information to hide in your puzzle, but you must not repeat information that you used in Step 3. DO NOT show where the words are. Fill up empty squares with random letters. Remember to keep a note of where your answers are hidden but do not show your friends. When you have a complete puzzle, exchange it with a friend to solve each other's puzzle.

Step 5

Now make up 10 questions (not "answers" this time) based on the same chapter used in the previous two tasks. Again, you must find NEW information that you have not yet used. Now it's getting hard to find that new information! Again, give your questions to a friend to answer.

Step 6

As you have been doing the puzzles, your brain has been actively searching for new information. Now write a NEW LIST that contains only the new information you have discovered when doing the puzzles. Your new list is the one to look at repeatedly for short bursts over the next few days. Try to remember more and more of it without looking at it. After a few days, you should be able to add words from your second list to your first list as you increase the information in your long-term memory.

FINALLY! Be inspired...

Make a list of different revision ideas and beside each one write **THINGS I HAVE** tried, **THINGS I WILL** try and **THINGS I MIGHT** try. Don't be scared of trying something new.

And remember – "FAIL TO PREPARE AND PREPARE TO FAIL!"

National 5 Mathematics

The course

The National 5 Mathematics course aims to enable you to develop the ability to:

- select and apply mathematical techniques in a variety of mathematical and real-life situations
- manipulate abstract terms in order to solve problems and to generalise
- interpret, communicate and manage information in mathematical form
- use mathematical language and explore mathematical ideas.

Before starting this course you should already have the knowledge, understanding and skills required to achieve a good pass in National 4 Mathematics and/or be proficient in equivalent experiences and outcomes. This course enables you to further develop your knowledge, understanding and skills in algebra, geometry, trigonometry, numeracy, statistics and reasoning. The course content is summarised below.

Algebra	Geometry	Trigonometry
• Expanding brackets • Factorising • Completing the square • Algebraic fractions • Equation of straight line • Equations and inequations • Simultaneous equations • Change of subject of formulae • Graphs of quadratic functions • Quadratic equations	• Gradient • Arc and sector of circle • Volume (including significant figures) • Pythagoras' theorem • Properties of shapes • Similarity • Vectors	• Graphs • Equations • Identities • Area of triangle, sine rule, cosine rule, bearings
	Numeracy	**Statistics**
	• Surds • Indices • Percentages • Fractions	• Semi-interquartile range, standard deviation • Scattergraphs; equation of line of best fit

Reasoning
• Interpreting a situation where mathematics can be used and identifying a strategy. • Explaining a solution and/or relating it to context.

Assessment

To gain the Course award, you must pass the three Units – Expressions & Formulae, Relationships and Applications – as well as the examination. The Units are assessed internally on a pass/fail basis and the examination is set and marked externally by the SQA. It tests skills beyond the minimum competence required for the Units.

The number of marks and the times allotted for the examination papers are as follows:

Paper 1 (non-calculator)	40 marks	1 hour
Paper 2	50 marks	1 hour 30 minutes

The Course award is graded A-D, the grade being determined by the total mark you score in the examination.

Some tips for achieving a good mark

- **DOING** maths questions is the most effective use of your study time. You will benefit much more from spending 30 minutes doing maths questions than spending several hours copying out notes or reading a maths textbook.

- Practise doing the type of questions that are likely to appear in the exam. Work through these practice papers and similar questions from past Credit Level and Intermediate 2 papers. Use the marking instructions to check your answers and to understand what the examiners are looking for. Ask your teacher for help if you get stuck.

- **SHOW ALL WORKING CLEARLY.** The instructions on the front of the exam paper state that "Full credit will only be given where the solution contains appropriate working". A "correct" answer with no working may only be awarded partial marks or even no marks at all. An incomplete answer will be awarded marks for any appropriate working. Attempt every question, even if you are not sure whether you are correct or not. Your solution may contain working which will gain some marks. A blank response is certain to be awarded no marks. Never score out working unless you have something better to replace it with.

- Communication is very important in presenting solutions to questions. Diagrams are often a good way of conveying information and enabling markers to understand your working. Where a diagram is included in a question, it is often good practice to copy it and show the results of your working on the copy.

- In Paper 1, you have to carry out calculations without a calculator. Candidates' performance in number skills is often disappointing, and costs many of them valuable marks. Ensure that you practise your number skills regularly, especially within questions testing Course content.
- In Paper 2, you will be allowed to use a calculator. Always use **your own** calculator. Different calculators often function in slightly different ways, so make sure that you know how to operate yours. Having to use a calculator that you are unfamiliar with on the day of the exam will disadvantage you.
- Prepare thoroughly to tackle questions from **all** parts of the course. Numerical and algebraic fractions, graphs of quadratic fractions, surds, indices and trigonometric identities are topics that often cause candidates problems. Be prepared to put extra effort into mastering these topics.

Some common errors to avoid

	Common error	Correct answer
Converse of Pythagoras' Theorem e.g. Prove that triangle ABC is right angled. 	Don't start by assuming what you are trying to prove is true. $AC^2 = AB^2 + BC^2$ $AC^2 = 3^2 + 4^2 = 9 + 16 = 25$ $AC = \sqrt{25} = 5$ so triangle ABC is right angled by the Converse of Pythagoras' Theorem.	Don't state that $AC^2 = AB^2 + BC^2$ until you have the evidence to prove that it is true. $AC^2 = 5^2 = 25$ $AB^2 + BC^2 = 3^2 + 4^2 = 9 + 16 = 25$ so $AC^2 = AB^2 + BC^2$ so triangle ABC is right angled by the Converse of Pythagoras' Theorem.
Similarity (area and volume) e.g. Theses cylinders are mathematically similar. The volume of the small one is $60cm^3$. Calculate the volume of the large one.	Don't use the linear scale factor to calculate the volume (or area) of a similar shape. Scale factor = 2 Volume = $2 \times 60 = 120cm^3$	Remember that volume factor = (linear factor)^3 area factor = (linear factor)^2 Scale factor = 2 Volume = $2^3 \times 60 = 480cm^3$
Reverse use of percentage e.g. After a 5% pay rise, Ann now earns £252 per week. Calculate her weekly pay before the rise.	Increase = 5% of old pay **NOT** 5% of new pay Increase = 5% of £252 = £12·60 Old pay = £252 - £12·60 = £239·40	New pay = (100% + 5%) of old pay New pay = 105% of old pay = £252 1% of old pay = £252 ÷ 105 = £2·40 Old pay = 100%= £2·40×100 =£240
Interpreting statistics e.g. Jack and Jill sat tests in the same eight subjects. Jack's mean mark was 76 and his standard deviation was 13. Jill's mean mark was 59 and her standard deviation was 21. Make two valid comments comparing the performance of Jack and Jill in the tests.	This answer does not show that you **understand** the meaning of mean and standard deviation. Jack has a higher mean mark but a lower standard deviation than Jill.	Your interpretation of the figures must show that you **understand** that mean is an average and that standard deviation is a measure of spread. On average Jack performed better than Jill as his mean mark was higher. Jack's performance was more consistent than Jill's as the standard deviation of his marks was lower.

Good luck!

Remember that the rewards for passing National 5 Mathematics are well worth it! Your pass will help you get the future you want for yourself. In the exam, be confident in your own ability, if you're not sure how to answer a question trust your instincts and just give it a go anyway – keep calm and don't panic! GOOD LUCK!

NATIONAL 5

Model Paper

Whilst this Model Paper has been specially commissioned by Hodder Gibson for use as practice for the National 5 exams, the key reference documents remain the SQA Specimen Paper 2013 and the SQA Past Papers 2014, 2015 and 2016.

HODDER
GIBSON
LEARN MORE

National
Qualifications
MODEL PAPER

Mathematics
Paper 1
(Non-Calculator)

Duration — 1 hour

Total marks — 40

You may NOT use a calculator.

Attempt ALL questions.

Use **blue** or **black** ink. Pencil may be used for graphs and diagrams only.

Write your working and answers in the spaces provided. Additional space for answers is provided at the end of this booklet. If you use this space, write clearly the number of the question you are attempting.

Square-ruled paper is provided at the back of this booklet.

Full credit will be given only to solutions which contain appropriate working.

State the units for your answer where appropriate.

Before leaving the examination room you must give this booklet to the Invigilator.
If you do not, you may lose all the marks for this paper.

FORMULAE LIST

The roots of $ax^2 + bx + c = 0$ are $x = \dfrac{-b \pm \sqrt{(b^2 - 4ac)}}{2a}$

Sine rule: $\dfrac{a}{\sin A} = \dfrac{b}{\sin B} = \dfrac{c}{\sin C}$

Cosine rule: $a^2 = b^2 + c^2 - 2bc\cos A$ or $\cos A = \dfrac{b^2 + c^2 - a^2}{2bc}$

Area of a triangle: $A = \dfrac{1}{2}ab\sin C$

Volume of a sphere: $V = \dfrac{4}{3}\pi r^3$

Volume of a cone: $V = \dfrac{1}{3}\pi r^2 h$

Volume of a pyramid: $V = \dfrac{1}{3}Ah$

Standard deviation: $s = \sqrt{\dfrac{\Sigma(x - \bar{x})^2}{n-1}} = \sqrt{\dfrac{\Sigma x^2 - (\Sigma x)^2/n}{n-1}}$, where n is the sample size.

MARKS | DO NOT WRITE IN THIS MARGIN

1. Evaluate

$$4\frac{1}{3} - 1\frac{1}{2}.$$

$\frac{13}{3} - \frac{3}{2}$ $\frac{26}{6} - \frac{9}{6} = \frac{17}{6}$ $2\frac{5}{6}$ (2)

2. Expand and simplify

$$(3x - 2)(2x^2 + x + 5).$$ (3)

$3x^3 + 3x^2 + 15x - 4x^2 - 2x - 10$

$3x^3 - x^2 + 13x - 10$ ✗

$6x^3 + 3x^2 + 5x - 4x^2 - 2x - 10$

$6x^3 - x^2 + 13x - 10$ ✓

3. Change the subject of the formula to m.

$$L = \frac{\sqrt{m}}{k}$$ 2

$Lk = \sqrt{m}$

$(L^2k) = \sqrt{m}$

$(Lk)^2 = m$

MARKS
DO NOT WRITE IN THIS MARGIN

4. The diagram shows a tiling of congruent triangles.

Vectors **u** and **v** are represented by $\overrightarrow{AB}$ and $\overrightarrow{AF}$ respectively.

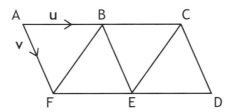

(a) Express $\overrightarrow{AD}$ in terms of **u** and **v**.

$2u + v$ ✓

(b) Express $\overrightarrow{CE}$ in terms of **u** and **v**.

$-u - v$ ✗ $v - u$

(1)

Total marks   2

5.

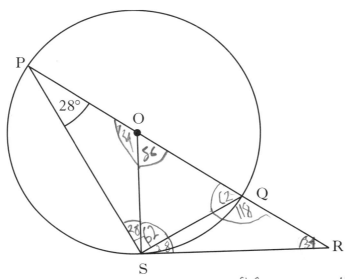

In the above diagram,

- O is the centre of the circle
- PQ is a diameter of the circle
- PQR is a straight line
- RS is a tangent to the circle at S
- angle QPS is 28°.

Calculate the size of angle QRS.

$\begin{array}{r} 90 \\ -\ 62 \\ \hline 28 \end{array}$

$\begin{array}{r} 118 \\ +\ 28 \\ \hline 146 \end{array}$

$\begin{array}{r} 180 \\ -146 \\ \hline 34 \end{array}$

$\begin{array}{r} 180 \\ -118 \\ \hline 62 \end{array}$

$34°$ ✓

(3)

MARKS | DO NOT WRITE IN THIS MARGIN

6. Express $\dfrac{3y^2 - 6y}{y^2 + y - 6}$ in its simplest form.　　　　3

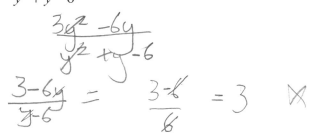

$$\frac{3y^2 - 6y}{y^2 + y - 6}$$

$$\frac{3 - 6y}{y - 6} = \frac{3 - 6}{6} = 3 \quad \cancel{\times}$$

7. Evaluate $9^{\frac{3}{2}}$.　　　　2

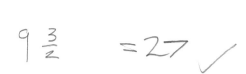

$$9^{\frac{3}{2}} \qquad = 27 \checkmark$$

8. The diagram shows part of the graph of $y = 5 + 4x - x^2$.

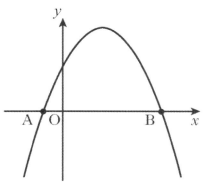

$$y = 5 + 4x - x^2$$

A is the point (-1, 0).

B is the point (5, 0).

(a) State the equation of the axis of symmetry of the graph.　　　　2

$$x = \frac{5 + -1}{}$$
$$x = 4 \div 2$$
$$x = 2 \checkmark$$

(b) Hence, find the maximum value of $y = 5 + 4x - x^2$.　　　　2

$$y = 5 + 4 \cdot 2 \cdot 2^2$$
$$y = 5 + 8 - 4$$
$$y = 9 \checkmark$$

Total marks 4

Page five

9. The graph below shows two straight lines.

- $y = 2x - 3$

- $x + 2y = 14$

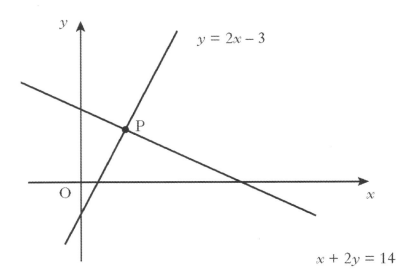

The lines intersect at the point P.

Find, **algebraically**, the coordinates of P.

4

$y = 2x - 3$

$14 = x + 2y$

$3 = 2x - y \quad \times 1$

$14 = x + 2y \quad \times 2$

$3 = 2x - y$

$28 = 2x + 4y$

$-\left(\begin{matrix} 3 = -y \\ 28 = 4y \end{matrix}\right)-$

$-25 = -5y$

$y = \dfrac{-25}{-5}$

$y = 5$

$14 = x + 2y$

$14 = x + 2 \times 5$

$14 = x + 10$

$14 = 4 + 10$

$x = 4$

Page six

MARKS | DO NOT WRITE IN THIS MARGIN

10. Part of the graph of $y = a \cos bx^o$ is shown in the diagram.

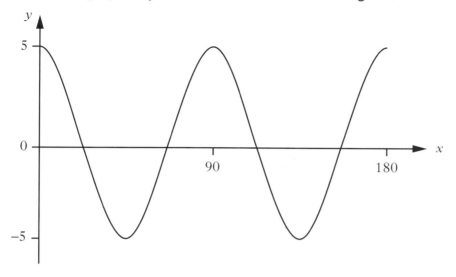

State the values of a and b.

2

$a = 5$

$b = 24$

11.

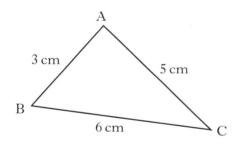

In triangle ABC, show that $\cos B = \dfrac{5}{9}$.

3

$\cos B = \dfrac{b^2 + c^2 - a^2}{2ab}$

$\cos B = \dfrac{5^2 + 3^2 - 6^2}{2 \times 6 \times 5}$

$\cos B = \dfrac{25 + 9 - 36}{60}$

$\cos B = 7$

MARKS

12.

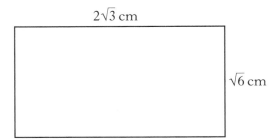

$2\sqrt{3}$ cm

$\sqrt{6}$ cm

The rectangle above has length $2\sqrt{3}$ centimetres and breadth $\sqrt{6}$ centimetres.

Calculate the area of the rectangle.

Express your answer as a surd in its simplest form.   **3**

$$2\sqrt{3} \times \sqrt{6}$$

$$= 2\sqrt{18}$$
$$= 2 \times \sqrt{9} \times \sqrt{2}$$
$$= 2 \times 3\sqrt{2}$$
$$= 6\sqrt{2} \checkmark$$

13. Simplify $\dfrac{3}{m}+\dfrac{4}{m+1}$.   **3**

$$\frac{3}{m}+\frac{4}{m+1} = \frac{3(m+1)}{m(m+1)}+\frac{4m}{m(m+1)} = \frac{3m+3}{m(m+1)}+\frac{4m}{m(m+1)}$$

$$\frac{7m+3}{m(m+1)} \checkmark$$

14. Prove that the roots of the equation $2x^2+8x+5=0$ are real and irrational.   **4**

$$2x^2+8x+5=0$$
$$(2x+4)(x^2+1)$$

$$2x^2+$$

[END OF MODEL PAPER]

ADDITIONAL SPACE FOR ANSWERS

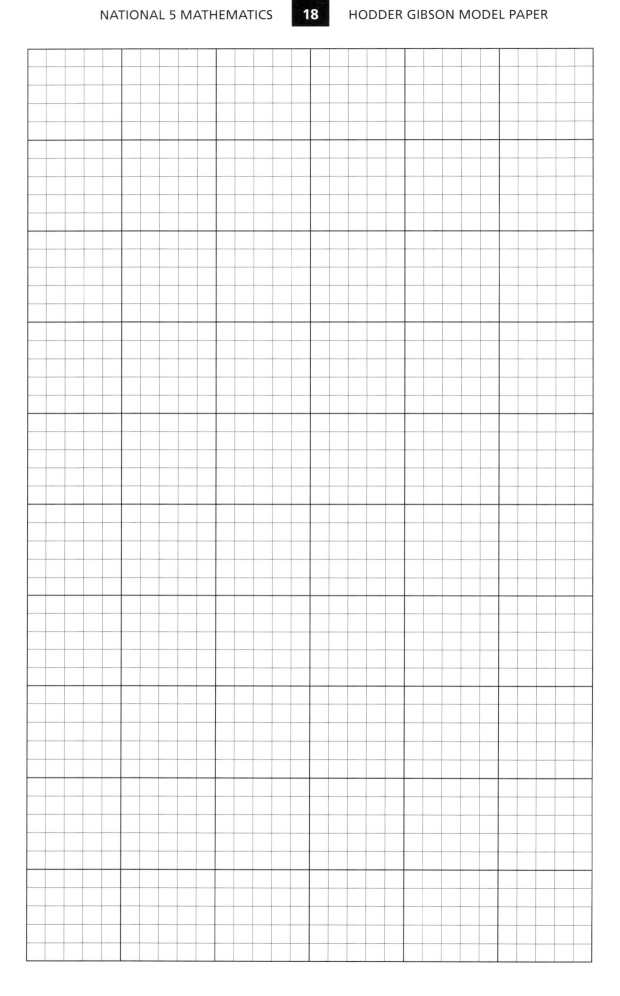

National
Qualifications
MODEL PAPER

Mathematics
Paper 2

Duration — 1 hour and 30 minutes

Total marks — 50

You may use a calculator.

Attempt ALL questions.

Use **blue** or **black** ink. Pencil may be used for graphs and diagrams only.

Write your working and answers in the spaces provided. Additional space for answers is provided at the end of this booklet. If you use this space, write clearly the number of the question you are attempting.

Square-ruled paper is provided at the back of this booklet.

Full credit will be given only to solutions which contain appropriate working.

State the units for your answer where appropriate.

Before leaving the examination room you must give this booklet to the Invigilator. If you do not, you may lose all the marks for this paper.

HODDER
GIBSON
LEARN MORE

FORMULAE LIST

The roots of $ax^2 + bx + c = 0$ are $x = \dfrac{-b \pm \sqrt{(b^2 - 4ac)}}{2a}$

Sine rule: $\dfrac{a}{\sin A} = \dfrac{b}{\sin B} = \dfrac{c}{\sin C}$

Cosine rule: $a^2 = b^2 + c^2 - 2bc\cos A$ or $\cos A = \dfrac{b^2 + c^2 - a^2}{2bc}$

Area of a triangle: $A = \dfrac{1}{2}ab\sin C$

Volume of a sphere: $V = \dfrac{4}{3}\pi r^3$

Volume of a cone: $V = \dfrac{1}{3}\pi r^2 h$

Volume of a pyramid: $V = \dfrac{1}{3}Ah$

Standard deviation: $s = \sqrt{\dfrac{\Sigma(x - \bar{x})^2}{n-1}} = \sqrt{\dfrac{\Sigma x^2 - (\Sigma x)^2/n}{n-1}}$, where n is the sample size.

MARKS | DO NOT WRITE IN THIS MARGIN

1. Alistair buys an antique chair for £600.

   It is expected to increase in value at the rate of 4·5% each year.

   How much is it expected to be worth in 3 years?   3

$$600 \times 1\cdot045^3 = x$$

$$x = £684 \cdot 699675$$

$$£ 684 \cdot 69$$

2. A rugby team scored the following points in a series of matches.

   13   7   0   9   7   8   5

   (a) For this sample calculate the mean and the standard deviation.   3

$$(13 + 7 + 0 + 9 + 7 + 8 + 5) \div 7 = 7$$

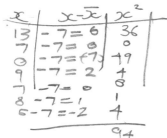

x	$x - \bar{x}$	x^2
13	$-7 = 6$	36
7	$-7 = 0$	0
0	$-7 = (-7)$	49
9	$-7 = 2$	4
7	$-7 = 0$	0
8	$-7 = 1$	1
5	$-7 = -2$	4
		94

$$S.D = \sqrt{\frac{94}{6}}$$

$$S.D = 3\cdot95814029$$

$$S.D = 4$$

The following season the team appoints a new coach.

A similar series of matches produces a mean of 27 and a standard deviation of 3·25.

   (b) Make two valid comparisons about the performance of the team under the new coach.   2

   Total marks   5

On average, under the new coach the team are scoring more points more consistently

35/50

MARKS | DO NOT WRITE IN THIS MARGIN

3. The diagram shows a cuboid OPQR,STUV relative to the coordinate axes.

   P is the point (4, 0, 0), Q is (4, 2, 0) and U is (4, 2, 3).

   M is the midpoint of OR.

   N is the point on UQ such that UN = $\frac{1}{3}$ UQ.

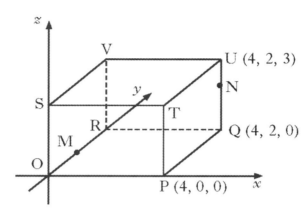

   State the coordinates of M and N.   2

   $$M = (0, 1, 0) \quad N(4, 2, 2)$$

4. Find the equation of the straight line shown in the diagram.

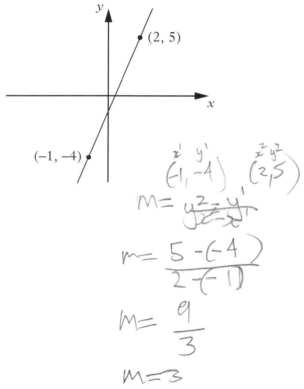

   (2, 5)

   (−1, −4)

   $$(-1, -4) \quad (2, 5)$$
   $$M = \frac{y^2 - y^1}{x^2 - x^1}$$
   $$m = \frac{5 - (-4)}{2 - (-1)}$$
   $$M = \frac{9}{3}$$
   $$M = 3$$

   $$y - 6 = m(x - a)$$
   $$y - 5 = 3(x - 2)$$
   $$y - 5 = 3x - 6$$
   $$y = 3x - 1$$

   3

MARKS | DO NOT WRITE IN THIS MARGIN

5. A spiral staircase is being designed.

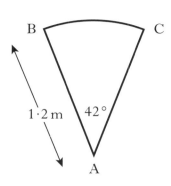

Each step is made from a sector of a circle as shown.

The radius is 1·2 metres.

Angle BAC is 42°.

For the staircase to pass safety regulations, the arc BC must be at least 0·9 metres.

Will the staircase pass safety regulations?

(4)

$$x = \frac{42}{360} \times \pi \times 2 \cdot 4$$

$$x = 0.8796459473 \, m^2$$

$$x = 0.88 \, m^2$$

this won't Pass safety regulations

6. A glass ornament is in the shape of a cone partly filled with coloured water.

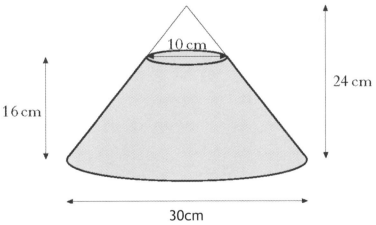

The cone is 24 centimetres high and has a base of diameter 30 centimetres.

The water is 16 centimetres deep and measures 10 centimetres across the top.

What is the volume of the water?

Give your answer **correct to 2 significant figures.**

(5)

Vol of large cone = $\frac{1}{3} \times \pi \times r^2 \times h$

$V = 5654.866776 \, cm^3$

subtract heights

Vol of small cone = 418.8790026

volume of water = $\frac{5654.8667}{418.87900}$
$\overline{5235.987786 cm}$

MARKS

7. The price for Paul's summer holiday is £894·40.

The price includes a 4% booking fee.

What is the price of his holiday without the booking fee?

3

£894·40 = 104%.

100% = 894·40 ÷ 100 × 4 = 35·776

894·400
− 35·776   £858·62
£858·624

8. A heavy metal beam, AB, rests against a vertical wall as shown.

The length of the beam is 8 metres and it makes and angle of 59° with the ground.

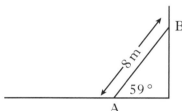

A cable, CB, is fixed to the ground at C and is attached to the top of the beam at B.

The cable makes an angle of 22° with the ground.

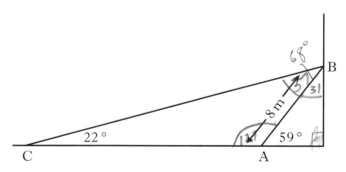

Calculate the length of cable CB.

4

−180
59 + 90 = 49
031°

$\dfrac{a}{\sin A} = \dfrac{b}{\sin b}$

$\dfrac{8}{\sin(22)} \times \dfrac{b}{\sin(127)}$

$L = \dfrac{8 \times \sin(127)}{\sin(22)}$

L = 17·0554 cm
b = 17 cm
b = 18·3cm

9. A necklace is made of beads which are mathematically similar.

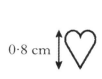 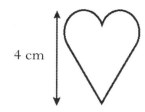 

0·8 cm

4 cm

The height of the smaller bead is 0·8 centimetres and its area is 0·6 square centimetres.
The height of the larger bead is 4 centimetres.
Find the area of the larger bead.

3

area = 0·6
height = 0·8

$\begin{array}{r} 0.6 \\ \overline{0.8} \\ \hline 0.75 \end{array}$

height = 4

area = 3 cm²

10. Paving stones are in the shape of a rhombus.

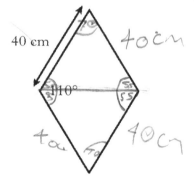

40 cm   40 cm

110°

40 cm   40 cm

$\begin{array}{r} 8c \\ -110 \\ \hline 7c \end{array}$

The side of each rhombus is 40 centimetres long.

The obtuse angle is 110°.

Find the area of one paving stone.

4

Area 1/2 ab sinc

Area = 1/2 40 × 40 × sin(70)

Area = 751.7540966 cm²
× 2
Area = 1503.508193

Area = 1503.5 cm³

MARKS

11. $f(x) = 3\sin x°, \quad 0 \le x \le 360.$

(a) Find $f(270)$.

1

$$f(270) = 3\sin(270) \quad f(270) = (-3)$$

(b) $f(t) = 0·6.$

Find the two possible values of t.

4

Total marks   5

12. A tanker delivers oil to garages.

The tanker has a circular cross-section as shown in the diagram below.

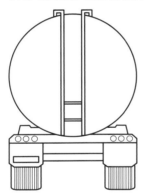
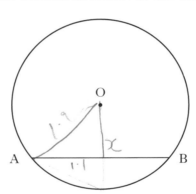

The radius of the circle, O, is 1·9 metres.

The width of the surface of the oil, represented by AB in the diagram, is 2·2 metres.

Calculate the depth of the oil in the tanker.

4

$$1·9^2 - 1·1^2 = x^2$$

$$x^2 = \sqrt{2·4}$$

$$x = 1·54919338\,m$$

$$x = 1·55m$$

$$\begin{array}{r} 1·9\,\text{?} \\ -1·9\end{array}$$

$$\begin{array}{r} 1·9\beta \\ -1·55 \\ \hline 0·35\,\text{?} \end{array}$$

MARKS | DO NOT WRITE IN THIS MARGIN

13. Triangles PQR and STU are mathematically similar.

The scale factor is 3 and PR corresponds to SU.

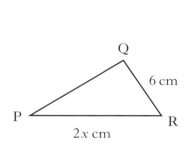
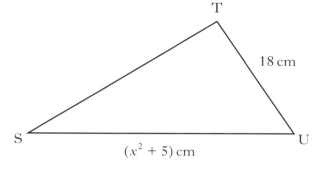

(a) Show that $x^2 - 6x + 5 = 0$.   **2**

$$x^2 - 6x + 5 = 0$$
$$x^2 - 6x = -5$$
$$5^2 - (6 \times 5) = -5$$
$$25 - 30 + 5 = 0$$

(b) Given that QR is the shortest side of triangle PQR, find the value of x.   **3**

Total marks   **5**

$$2x > 6$$

[END OF MODEL PAPER]

ADDITIONAL SPACE FOR ANSWERS

Page ten

ADDITIONAL SPACE FOR ANSWERS

Page eleven

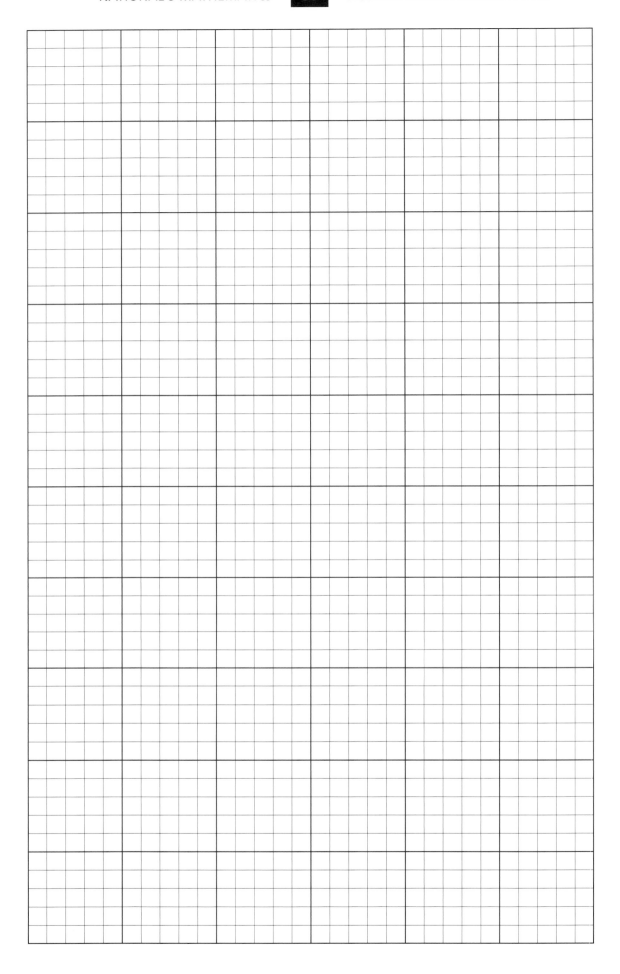

NATIONAL 5

2014

N5

National Qualifications 2014

Mark

X747/75/01

Mathematics
Paper 1
(Non-Calculator)

TUESDAY, 06 MAY

9:00 AM — 10:00 AM

Fill in these boxes and read what is printed below.

Full name of centre

Town

Forename(s)

Surname

Number of seat

Date of birth

Day	Month	Year
D D	M M	Y Y

Scottish candidate number

Total marks — 40

Attempt ALL questions.

Write your answers clearly in the spaces provided in this booklet. Additional space for answers is provided at the end of this booklet. If you use this space you must clearly identify the question number you are attempting.

Use **blue** or **black** ink.

You may NOT use a calculator.

Full credit will be given only to solutions which contain appropriate working.

State the units for your answer where appropriate.

Before leaving the examination room you must give this booklet to the Invigilator; if you do not, you may lose all the marks for this paper.

FORMULAE LIST

The roots of $ax^2 + bx + c = 0$ are $x = \dfrac{-b \pm \sqrt{(b^2 - 4ac)}}{2a}$

Sine rule: $\dfrac{a}{\sin A} = \dfrac{b}{\sin B} = \dfrac{c}{\sin C}$

Cosine rule: $a^2 = b^2 + c^2 - 2bc \cos A$ or $\cos A = \dfrac{b^2 + c^2 - a^2}{2bc}$

Area of a triangle: $A = \dfrac{1}{2} ab \sin C$

Volume of a sphere: $V = \dfrac{4}{3} \pi r^3$

Volume of a cone: $V = \dfrac{1}{3} \pi r^2 h$

Volume of a pyramid: $V = \dfrac{1}{3} Ah$

Standard deviation: $s = \sqrt{\dfrac{\Sigma(x - \bar{x})^2}{n-1}} = \sqrt{\dfrac{\Sigma x^2 - (\Sigma x)^2 / n}{n-1}}$, where n is the sample size.

MARKS

DO NOT WRITE IN THIS MARGIN

1. Evaluate $\dfrac{5}{12} \times 2\dfrac{2}{9}$.

   Give the answer in simplest form.

   2

$$\frac{25}{27}$$

2. Multiply out the brackets and collect like terms:

   $(2x-5)(3x+1)$.

   2

$(2x-5)(3x+1)$

$6x^2 \; 2x +5x -5$

$6x^2 \; -13x -5$

[Turn over

3. Express $x^2 - 14x + 44$ in the form $(x - a)^2 + b$.

2

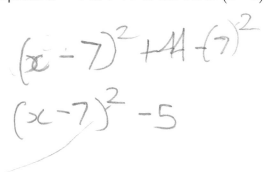

$$(x - 7)^2 + 44 - (7)^2$$

$$(x - 7)^2 - 5$$

4. Find the resultant vector $2u - v$ when $u = \begin{pmatrix} -2 \\ 3 \\ 5 \end{pmatrix}$ and $v = \begin{pmatrix} 0 \\ -4 \\ 7 \end{pmatrix}$.

Express your answer in component form.

2

$$2u - v \quad \begin{pmatrix} -4 \\ 6 \\ 10 \end{pmatrix} - \begin{pmatrix} 0 \\ (-4) \\ 7 \end{pmatrix}$$

$$\begin{pmatrix} -4 \\ 10 \\ 3 \end{pmatrix}$$

MARKS

DO NOT
WRITE IN
THIS
MARGIN

5. In triangle KLM

- KM = 18 centimetres
- sin K = 0·4
- sin L = 0·9

Calculate the length of LM.

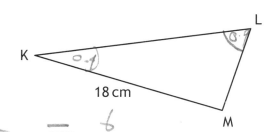

3

$$\frac{a}{Sin A} = \frac{b}{Sin B}$$

$$\frac{18}{0.9} = \frac{?}{0.4}$$

$$\frac{18 \times Sin(0.4)}{Sin(0.9)} = 8.00 \, cm$$

[Turn over

MARKS

6. McGregor's Burgers sells fast food.

The graph shows the relationship between the amount of fat, *F* grams, and the number of calories, *C*, in some of their sandwiches.

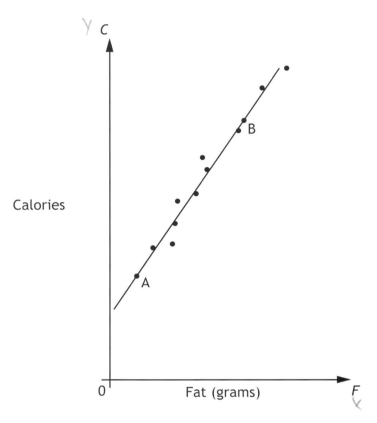

A line of best fit has been drawn.

Point A represents a sandwich which has 5 grams of fat and 200 calories.

Point B represents a sandwich which has 25 grams of fat and 500 calories.

MARKS

DO NOT WRITE IN THIS MARGIN

6. (continued)

(a) Find the equation of the line of best fit in terms of F and C.

3

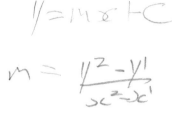

$$y = mx + c$$

$$m = \frac{y_2 - y_1}{x_2 - x_1} \qquad \underset{(200,5)}{\overset{x_1 \; y_1}{}} \underset{(500, 25)}{\overset{x_2 \; y_2}{}}$$

$$m = \frac{25 - 5}{500 - 200}$$

$$y - b = m(x - a)$$

$$m = \frac{20}{300} \qquad y - 200 = 15(x - 5)$$

$$M = 0.666666667 \qquad y - = 15x - 75$$

$$y = 15x + 65$$

(b) A Super Deluxe sandwich contains 40 grams of fat.

Use your answer to part (a) to estimate the number of calories this sandwich contains.

Show your working.

1

$$\times 8 \; (60 - 5) \times 8$$

$$480 \div 40$$

480 cal.

$$y = 15x + 125$$

$$y = 15x + 125$$

$$y = 625 \; cal$$

725 cal

Total marks 4

[Turn over

MARKS | DO NOT WRITE IN THIS MARGIN

7. The diagram below shows part of the graph of $y = ax^2$

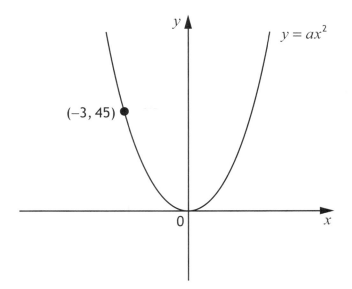

Find the value of a.   2

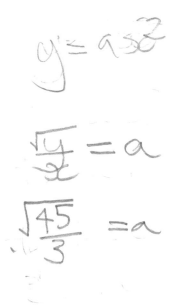

$$y = ax^2$$

$$\sqrt{\frac{y}{x}} = a$$

$$\sqrt{\frac{45}{3}} = a$$

MARKS

8. Express $\sqrt{40} + 4\sqrt{10} + \sqrt{90}$ as a surd in its simplest form.   3

9. 480 000 tickets were sold for a tennis tournament last year.

    This represents 80% of all the available tickets.

    Calculate the total number of tickets that were available for this tournament.   3

[Turn over

MARKS | DO NOT WRITE IN THIS MARGIN

10. The graph of $y = a \sin (x + b)°$, $0 \leq x \leq 360$, is shown below.

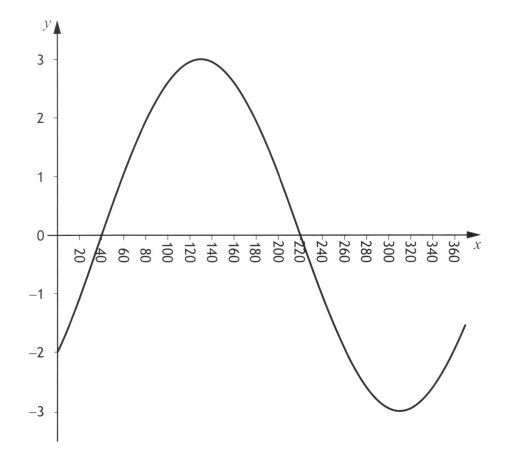

Write down the values of a and b.

2

MARKS DO NOT WRITE IN THIS MARGIN

11. (a) A straight line has equation $4x + 3y = 12$.

Find the gradient of this line. **2**

(b) Find the coordinates of the point where this line crosses the x-axis. **2**

Total marks 4

[Turn over

MARKS | DO NOT WRITE IN THIS MARGIN

12. The diagram below shows a circle, centre C.

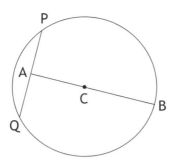

The radius of the circle is 15 centimetres.

A is the mid-point of chord PQ.

The length of AB is 27 centimetres.

Calculate the length of PQ.

4

MARKS | DO NOT WRITE IN THIS MARGIN

13. The diagram below shows the path of a small rocket which is fired into the air. The height, h metres, of the rocket after t seconds is given by

$$h(t) = 16t - t^2$$

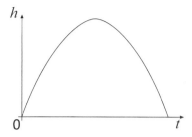

(a) After how many seconds will the rocket first be at a height of 60 metres?   **4**

(b) Will the rocket reach a height of 70 metres?
Justify your answer.   **3**

Total marks   **7**

[END OF QUESTION PAPER]

MARKS DO NOT WRITE IN THIS MARGIN

ADDITIONAL SPACE FOR ANSWERS

MARKS | DO NOT WRITE IN THIS MARGIN

ADDITIONAL SPACE FOR ANSWERS

Page fifteen

[BLANK PAGE]

DO NOT WRITE ON THIS PAGE

N5

National
Qualifications
2014

Mark

X747/75/02

Mathematics
Paper 2

TUESDAY, 06 MAY

10:20 AM — 11:50 AM

Fill in these boxes and read what is printed below.

Full name of centre

Town

Forename(s)

Surname

Number of seat

Date of birth

Day	Month	Year
D D	M M	Y Y

Scottish candidate number

Total marks — 50

Attempt ALL questions.

Write your answers clearly in the spaces provided in this booklet. Additional space for answers is provided at the end of this booklet. If you use this space you must clearly identify the question number you are attempting.

Use **blue** or **black** ink.

You may use a calculator.

Full credit will be given only to solutions which contain appropriate working.

State the units for your answer where appropriate.

Before leaving the examination room you must give this booklet to the Invigilator; if you do not, you may lose all the marks for this paper.

FORMULAE LIST

The roots of $ax^2 + bx + c = 0$ are $x = \dfrac{-b \pm \sqrt{(b^2 - 4ac)}}{2a}$

Sine rule: $\dfrac{a}{\sin A} = \dfrac{b}{\sin B} = \dfrac{c}{\sin C}$

Cosine rule: $a^2 = b^2 + c^2 - 2bc \cos A$ or $\cos A = \dfrac{b^2 + c^2 - a^2}{2bc}$

Area of a triangle: $A = \dfrac{1}{2}ab \sin C$

Volume of a sphere: $V = \dfrac{4}{3}\pi r^3$

Volume of a cone: $V = \dfrac{1}{3}\pi r^2 h$

Volume of a pyramid: $V = \dfrac{1}{3}Ah$

Standard deviation: $s = \sqrt{\dfrac{\Sigma(x - \bar{x})^2}{n-1}} = \sqrt{\dfrac{\Sigma x^2 - (\Sigma x)^2/n}{n-1}}$, where n is the sample size.

1. There are 964 pupils on the roll of Aberleven High School.

   It is forecast that the roll will decrease by 15% per year.

   What will be the expected roll after 3 years?

   Give your answer to the nearest ten.   3

[Turn over

MARKS

2. The diagram shows a cube placed on top of a cuboid, relative to the coordinate axes.

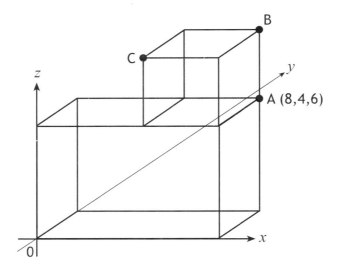

A is the point (8,4,6).

Write down the coordinates of B and C.

2

MARKS

DO NOT WRITE IN THIS MARGIN

3. Two groups of people go to a theatre.

Bill buys tickets for 5 adults and 3 children.

The total cost of his tickets is £158·25.

(a) Write down an equation to illustrate this information.   1

(b) Ben buys tickets for 3 adults and 2 children.

The total cost of his tickets is £98.

Write down an equation to illustrate this information.   1

(c) Calculate the cost of a ticket for an adult and the cost of a ticket for a child.   4

Total marks   6

[Turn over

MARKS

4. A runner has recorded her times, in seconds, for six different laps of a running track.

53   57   58   60   55   56

(a)   (i)   Calculate the mean of these lap times.

Show clearly all your working.   1

(ii)   Calculate the standard deviation of these lap times.

Show clearly all your working.   3

MARKS | DO NOT WRITE IN THIS MARGIN

4. **(continued)**

(b) She changes her training routine hoping to improve her consistency.

After this change, she records her times for another six laps.

The mean is 55 seconds and the standard deviation 3·2 seconds.

Has the new training routine improved her consistency?

Give a reason for your answer.   1

Total marks   5

[Turn over

MARKS

5. A supermarket sells cylindrical cookie jars which are mathematically similar.

The smaller jar has a height of 15 centimetres and a volume of 750 cubic centimetres.

The larger jar has a height of 24 centimetres.

Calculate the volume of the larger jar.   3

MARKS

6. The diagram below shows the position of three towns.

Lowtown is due west of Midtown.

The distance from

- Lowtown to Midtown is 75 kilometres.
- Midtown to Hightown is 110 kilometres.
- Hightown to Lowtown is 85 kilometres.

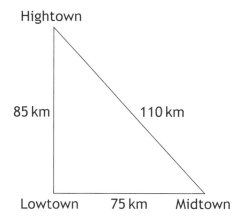

Is Hightown directly north of Lowtown?

Justify your answer.   4

[Turn over

MARKS | DO NOT WRITE IN THIS MARGIN

7. An ornament is in the shape of a cone with diameter 8 centimetres and height 15 centimetres.

The bottom contains a hemisphere made of copper with diameter 7·4 centimetres. The rest is made of glass, as shown in the diagram below.

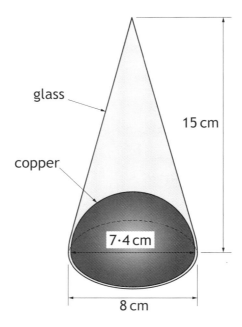

glass

15 cm

copper

7·4 cm

8 cm

Calculate the volume of the glass part of the ornament.

Give your answer correct to 2 significant figures.

5

MARKS | DO NOT WRITE IN THIS MARGIN

8. Simplify $\dfrac{n^5 \times 10n}{2n^2}$.

3

9. Express $\dfrac{7}{x+5} - \dfrac{3}{x}$ $\quad x \neq -5, \ x \neq 0$ as a single fraction in its simplest form.

3

[Turn over

MARKS | DO NOT WRITE IN THIS MARGIN

10. In a race, boats sail round three buoys represented by A, B, and C in the diagram below.

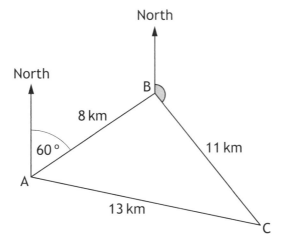

B is 8 kilometres from A on a bearing of 060°.

C is 11 kilometres from B.

A is 13 kilometres from C.

(a) Calculate the size of angle ABC.   3

(b) Hence find the size of the shaded angle.   2

Total marks   5

MARKS | DO NOT WRITE IN THIS MARGIN

11. Change the subject of the formula $s = ut + \frac{1}{2}at^2$ to a.   3

12. Solve the equation $11\cos x° - 2 = 3$, for $0 \leq x \leq 360$.   3

[Turn over

MARKS | DO NOT WRITE IN THIS MARGIN

13. The picture shows the entrance to a tunnel which is in the shape of part of a circle.

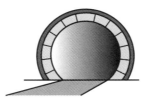

The diagram below represents the cross-section of the tunnel.

- The centre of the circle is O.

- MN is a chord of the circle.

- Angle MON is 50°.

- The radius of the circle is 7 metres.

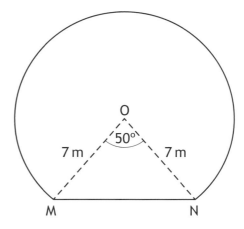

Calculate the area of the cross-section of the tunnel. 5

[END OF QUESTION PAPER]

MARKS

ADDITIONAL SPACE FOR ANSWERS

MARKS DO NOT WRITE IN THIS MARGIN

ADDITIONAL SPACE FOR ANSWERS

NATIONAL 5

2015

N5

National
Qualifications
2015

Mark

X747/75/01

Mathematics
Paper 1
(Non-Calculator)

TUESDAY, 19 MAY

9:00 AM — 10:00 AM

Fill in these boxes and read what is printed below.

Full name of centre

Town

Forename(s)

Surname

Number of seat

Date of birth

Day	Month	Year

Scottish candidate number

Total marks — 40

Attempt ALL questions.

You may NOT use a calculator.

Full credit will be given only to solutions which contain appropriate working.

State the units for your answer where appropriate.

Write your answers clearly in the spaces provided in this booklet. Additional space for answers is provided at the end of this booklet. If you use this space you must clearly identify the question number you are attempting.

Use **blue** or **black** ink.

Before leaving the examination room you must give this booklet to the Invigilator; if you do not, you may lose all the marks for this paper.

SQA

FORMULAE LIST

The roots of $ax^2 + bx + c = 0$ are $x = \dfrac{-b \pm \sqrt{(b^2 - 4ac)}}{2a}$

Sine rule: $\dfrac{a}{\sin A} = \dfrac{b}{\sin B} = \dfrac{c}{\sin C}$

Cosine rule: $a^2 = b^2 + c^2 - 2bc \cos A$ or $\cos A = \dfrac{b^2 + c^2 - a^2}{2bc}$

Area of a triangle: $A = \dfrac{1}{2} ab \sin C$

Volume of a sphere: $V = \dfrac{4}{3} \pi r^3$

Volume of a cone: $V = \dfrac{1}{3} \pi r^2 h$

Volume of a pyramid: $V = \dfrac{1}{3} Ah$

Standard deviation: $s = \sqrt{\dfrac{\Sigma(x - \bar{x})^2}{n-1}} = \sqrt{\dfrac{\Sigma x^2 - (\Sigma x)^2 / n}{n-1}}$, where n is the sample size.

MARKS |

1. Evaluate $6\frac{1}{5} - 2\frac{1}{3}$.

2

2. Solve algebraically the inequality

$$11 - 2(1 + 3x) < 39$$

3

$11 - 2 - 6x < 39$

$-2 - 6x < 28$

$-6x < 30$

$x < \dfrac{30}{6}$

$x < 5$

$-6x = 30$

$x = 30/-6$

$x = -5$

$-6x < 30$

$x > -5$

[Turn over

wrong

$\times$ $-6x < 30$

$x < 30/-6$

< -5

MARKS

DO NOT WRITE IN THIS MARGIN

3.

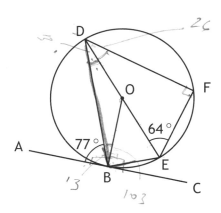

AC is a tangent to the circle, centre O, with point of contact B.

DE is a diameter of the circle and F is a point on the circumference.

Angle ABD is 77° and angle DEF is 64°.

Calculate the size of angle BDF.

3

4. Multiply out the brackets and collect like terms

$$(x-4)(x^2+x-2).$$

3

$x^3 + x^2 - 2x - 4x^2 - 4x + 8$

$x^3 - 3x^2 - 6x + 8$

MARKS | DO NOT WRITE IN THIS MARGIN

5. The standard deviation of 1, 2, 2, 2, 8 is equal to $\sqrt{a}$.

Find the value of a.

3

$15 - 5 = 3$

			$\dfrac{x^2}{25}$
8	-3	$=5$	
2	-3	$=-1$	1
2	-3	$=-1$	1
2	-3	$=-1$	1
1	-3	$=-2$	4

$\overline{32}$

$\sqrt{\dfrac{32}{4}}$

$\sqrt{8}$

[Turn over

MARKS | DO NOT WRITE IN THIS MARGIN

6. Part of the graph of $y = a \sin bx°$ is shown in the diagram.

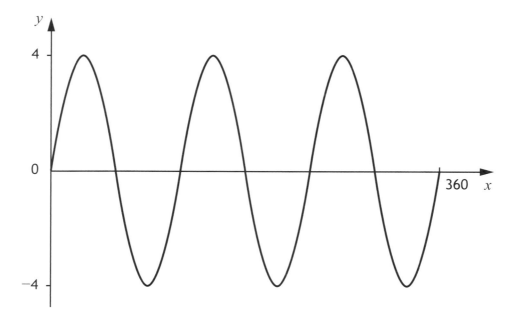

State the values of a and b.

2

MARKS | DO NOT WRITE IN THIS MARGIN

7. The graph below shows part of the parabola with equation of the form

$$y = (x + a)^2 + b.$$

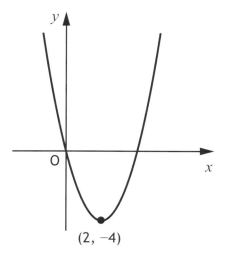

(2, −4)

The minimum turning point (2, −4) is shown in the diagram.

(a) State the values of

   (i) a 1

   (ii) b.   1

(b) Write down the equation of the axis of symmetry of the graph.   1

[Turn over

Page seven

MARKS

8. Find the equation of the line joining the points $(-2, 5)$ and $(3, 15)$.

   Give the equation in its simplest form.

   3

9. Write the following in order of size starting with the smallest.

   $$\cos 90° \qquad \cos 100° \qquad \cos 300°$$

   Justify your answer.

   2

MARKS | DO NOT WRITE IN THIS MARGIN

10. Ten couples took part in a dance competition.

The couples were given a score in each round.

The scores in the first round were

16   27   12   18   26   21   27   22   18   17

(a) Calculate the median and semi-interquartile range of these scores.   **3**

(b) In the second round, the median was 26 and the semi-interquartile range was 2·5.

Make two valid comparisons between the scores in the first and second rounds.   **2**

[Turn over

MARKS

11. Solve algebraically the system of equations

$$3x + 2y = 17$$
$$2x + 5y = 4.$$

3

MARKS

12. Simplify $\dfrac{x^2 - 4x}{x^2 + x - 20}$.

3

[Turn over for Question 13 on *Page twelve*

[Turn over

MARKS | DO NOT WRITE IN THIS MARGIN

13. Express $\dfrac{4}{\sqrt{8}}$ with a rational denominator.

Give your answer in its simplest form.   3

14. Evaluate $8^{\frac{5}{3}}$.   2

[END OF QUESTION PAPER]

MARKS

ADDITIONAL SPACE FOR ANSWERS

MARKS

ADDITIONAL SPACE FOR ANSWERS

N5

National
Qualifications
2015

Mark

X747/75/02

Mathematics
Paper 2

TUESDAY, 19 MAY
10:20 AM — 11:50 AM

Fill in these boxes and read what is printed below.

Full name of centre

Town

Forename(s)

Surname

Number of seat

Date of birth

Day   Month   Year

Scottish candidate number

Total marks — 50

Attempt ALL questions.

You may use a calculator.

Full credit will be given only to solutions which contain appropriate working.

State the units for your answer where appropriate.

Write your answers clearly in the spaces provided in this booklet. Additional space for answers is provided at the end of this booklet. If you use this space you must clearly identify the question number you are attempting.

Use **blue** or **black** ink.

Before leaving the examination room you must give this booklet to the Invigilator; if you do not, you may lose all the marks for this paper.

FORMULAE LIST

The roots of $ax^2 + bx + c = 0$ are $x = \dfrac{-b \pm \sqrt{(b^2 - 4ac)}}{2a}$

Sine rule: $\dfrac{a}{\sin A} = \dfrac{b}{\sin B} = \dfrac{c}{\sin C}$

Cosine rule: $a^2 = b^2 + c^2 - 2bc\cos A$ or $\cos A = \dfrac{b^2 + c^2 - a^2}{2bc}$

Area of a triangle: $A = \dfrac{1}{2}ab\sin C$

Volume of a sphere: $V = \dfrac{4}{3}\pi r^3$

Volume of a cone: $V = \dfrac{1}{3}\pi r^2 h$

Volume of a pyramid: $V = \dfrac{1}{3}Ah$

Standard deviation: $s = \sqrt{\dfrac{\Sigma(x - \bar{x})^2}{n-1}} = \sqrt{\dfrac{\Sigma x^2 - (\Sigma x)^2 / n}{n-1}}$, where n is the sample size.

MARKS | DO NOT WRITE IN THIS MARGIN

1. A house is valued at £240 000.

Its value is predicted to rise by 2·8% per annum.

Calculate its predicted value after 2 years.   **3**

2. A function is defined as $f(x) = 3x + 2$.

Given that $f(a) = 23$, calculate a.   **2**

[Turn over

MARKS

3. Triangle ABC is shown below.

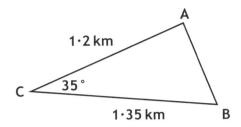

Calculate the length of AB.   3

MARKS DO NOT WRITE IN THIS MARGIN

4. Find $|\mathbf{u}|$, the magnitude of vector $\mathbf{u} = \begin{pmatrix} 6 \\ -13 \\ 18 \end{pmatrix}$. 2

[Turn over

MARKS

5. The vectors **p** and **q** are shown in the diagram below.

Find the resultant vector **p** + **q**.

Express your answer in component form.

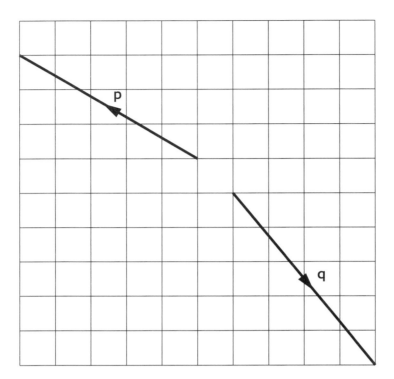

2

MARKS | DO NOT WRITE IN THIS MARGIN

6. (a)   The Earth is approximately spherical with a radius of 6400 kilometres.

Calculate the volume of the Earth giving your answer in scientific notation, correct to 2 significant figures.

3

(b)   The approximate volume of the Moon is $2 \cdot 2 \times 10^{10}$ cubic kilometres.

Calculate how many times the Earth's volume is greater than the Moon's.

2

[Turn over

MARKS | DO NOT WRITE IN THIS MARGIN

7. Express $\dfrac{5t}{s} \div \dfrac{t}{2s^2}$ in its simplest form.   **3**

8. James paid £297·50 for a laptop in a sale.

   The discount in the sale was 15%.

   Calculate the original price of the laptop.   **3**

MARKS | DO NOT WRITE IN THIS MARGIN

9. The flag at each hole on a golf course is coloured red and blue.

The diagram below represents a flag.

Triangle QRT represents the red section.

PQTS represents the blue section.

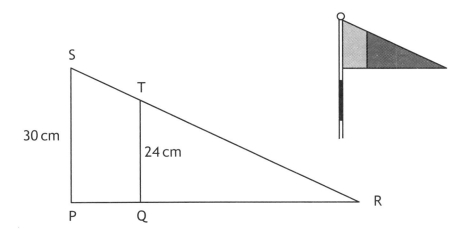

Triangles PRS and QRT are mathematically similar.

The area of triangle QRT is 400 square centimetres.

Calculate the area of PQTS, the blue section of the flag.   4

[Turn over

MARKS | DO NOT WRITE IN THIS MARGIN

10. The pendulum of a clock swings along an arc of a circle, centre O.

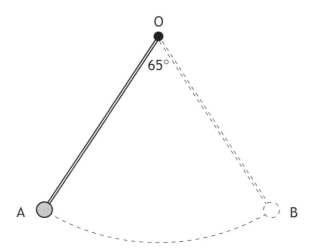

The pendulum swings through an angle of 65°, travelling from A to B.

The length of the arc AB is 28·4 centimetres.

Calculate the length of the pendulum.   4

MARKS

11. The top of a table is in the shape of a regular hexagon.

The three diagonals of the hexagon which are shown as dotted lines in the diagram below each have length 40 centimetres.

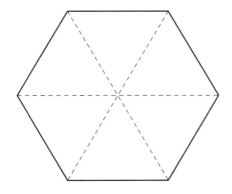

Calculate the area of the top of the table.   4

[Turn over

MARKS | DO NOT WRITE IN THIS MARGIN

12. The diagram below shows the circular cross-section of a milk tank.

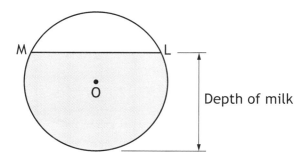

The radius of the circle, centre O, is 1·2 metres.

The width of the surface of the milk in the tank, represented by ML in the diagram, is 1·8 metres.

Calculate the depth of the milk in the tank.   4

MARKS

13. In the diagram below P, Q and R represent the positions of Portlee, Queenstown and Rushton respectively.

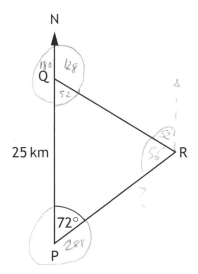

Portlee is 25 kilometres due South of Queenstown.
From Portlee, the bearing of Rushton is 072°.
From Queenstown, the bearing of Rushton is 128°.

Calculate the distance between Portlee and Rushton.

Do not use a scale drawing.

4

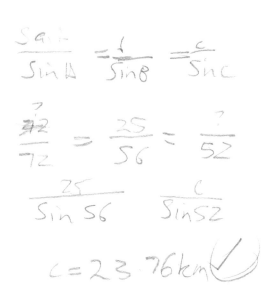

[Turn over

MARKS

DO NOT WRITE IN THIS MARGIN

14. A rectangular picture measuring 9 centimetres by 13 centimetres is placed on a rectangular piece of card.

The area of the card is 270 square centimetres.

There is a border x centimetres wide on all sides of the picture.

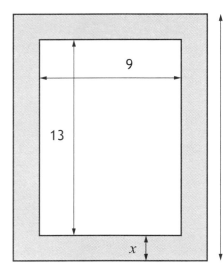

length

(a)   (i)   Write down an expression for the length of the card in terms of x.   1

area $= 270$ $x = length - 13$

area $= 117$

(ii)   Hence show that $4x^2 + 44x - 153 = 0$.   2

$4x^2 + 44x = 153$

$4x^2 + 44x - 153$

$x = \dfrac{-b \pm \sqrt{(b^2 - 4ac)}}{2a}$

$\dfrac{+44 \pm \sqrt{44^2 - 4 \times 4 \times (-153)}}{2 \times 4}$

MARKS

14. **(continued)**

(b) Calculate x, the width of the border.

Give your answer correct to one decimal place.   4

[END OF QUESTION PAPER]

MARKS

DO NOT
WRITE IN
THIS
MARGIN

ADDITIONAL SPACE FOR ANSWERS

ADDITIONAL SPACE FOR ANSWERS

[BLANK PAGE]

DO NOT WRITE ON THIS PAGE

NATIONAL 5

2016

N5

National Qualifications 2016

Mark

X747/75/01

Mathematics
Paper 1
(Non-Calculator)

THURSDAY, 12 MAY
1:00 PM — 2:00 PM

Fill in these boxes and read what is printed below.

Full name of centre

Town

Forename(s)

Surname

Number of seat

Date of birth

Day	Month	Year

Scottish candidate number

Total marks — 40

Attempt ALL questions.

You may NOT use a calculator.

Full credit will be given only to solutions which contain appropriate working.

State the units for your answer where appropriate.

Write your answers clearly in the spaces provided in this booklet. Additional space for answers is provided at the end of this booklet. If you use this space you must clearly identify the question number you are attempting.

Use **blue** or **black** ink.

Before leaving the examination room you must give this booklet to the Invigilator; if you do not, you may lose all the marks for this paper.

FORMULAE LIST

The roots of $ax^2 + bx + c = 0$ are $x = \dfrac{-b \pm \sqrt{(b^2 - 4ac)}}{2a}$

Sine rule: $\dfrac{a}{\sin A} = \dfrac{b}{\sin B} = \dfrac{c}{\sin C}$

Cosine rule: $a^2 = b^2 + c^2 - 2bc \cos A$ or $\cos A = \dfrac{b^2 + c^2 - a^2}{2bc}$

Area of a triangle: $A = \tfrac{1}{2} ab \sin C$

Volume of a sphere: $V = \tfrac{4}{3} \pi r^3$

Volume of a cone: $V = \tfrac{1}{3} \pi r^2 h$

Volume of a pyramid: $V = \tfrac{1}{3} Ah$

Standard deviation: $s = \sqrt{\dfrac{\Sigma(x - \bar{x})^2}{n-1}}$

or $s = \sqrt{\dfrac{\Sigma x^2 - \dfrac{(\Sigma x)^2}{n}}{n-1}}$, where n is the sample size.

MARKS | DO NOT WRITE IN THIS MARGIN

Total marks — 40

Attempt ALL questions

1. Given $\mathbf{p} = \begin{pmatrix} 4 \\ -6 \end{pmatrix}$ and $\mathbf{q} = \begin{pmatrix} -5 \\ -1 \end{pmatrix}$.

    Find the resultant vector $\frac{1}{2}\mathbf{p} + \mathbf{q}$.

    Express your answer in component form.   **2**

2. Evaluate $\frac{3}{4}\left(\frac{1}{3} + \frac{2}{7}\right)$.

    Give your answer in its simplest form.   **2**

[Turn over

MARKS | DO NOT WRITE IN THIS MARGIN

3. The diagram shows a sector of a circle, centre C.

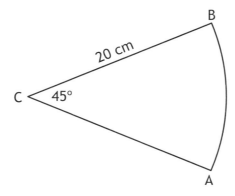

The radius of the circle is 20 centimetres and angle ACB is 45°.

Calculate the area of the sector.

Take π = 3·14.   3

MARKS | DO NOT WRITE IN THIS MARGIN

4. Charlie is making costumes for a school show.

One day he made 2 cloaks and 3 dresses.

The total amount of material he used was 9·6 square metres.

(a) Write down an equation to illustrate this information.   1

(b) The following day Charlie made 3 cloaks and 4 dresses.

The total amount of material he used was 13·3 square metres.

Write down an equation to illustrate this information.   1

(c) Calculate the amount of material required to make one cloak and the amount of material required to make one dress.   4

[Turn over

MARKS | DO NOT WRITE IN THIS MARGIN

5. A cattle farmer records the weight of some of his calves.

The scattergraph shows the relationship between the age, A months, and the weight, W kilograms, of the calves.

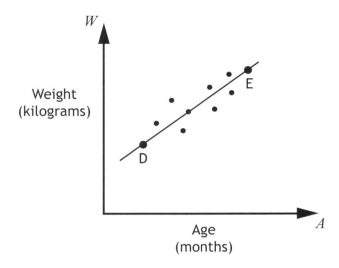

A line of best fit is drawn.

Point D represents a 3 month old calf which weighs 100 kilograms.

Point E represents a 15 month old calf which weighs 340 kilograms.

(a) Find the equation of the line of best fit in terms of A and W.
     Give the equation in its simplest form.   **3**

MARKS | DO NOT WRITE IN THIS MARGIN

5. (continued)

(b) Use your equation from part (a) to estimate the weight of a one **year** old calf.

Show your working.   1

6. Determine the nature of the roots of the function $f(x) = 7x^2 + 5x - 1$.   2

MARKS | DO NOT WRITE IN THIS MARGIN

7. The diagram shows a rectangular based pyramid, relative to the coordinate axes.

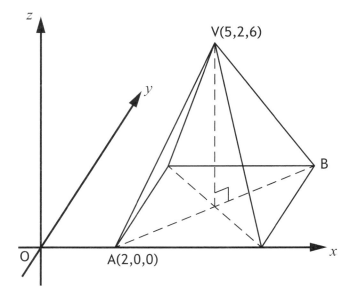

- A is the point (2,0,0).
- V is the point (5,2,6).

(a) Write down the coordinates of B.   1

(b) Calculate the length of edge AV of the pyramid.   3

MARKS · DO NOT WRITE IN THIS MARGIN

8. Solve the equation

$$\frac{2x}{3} - \frac{5}{6} = 2x.$$

   Give your answer in its simplest form.   3

9. The function $f(x)$ is defined by $f(x) = \dfrac{2}{\sqrt{x}}$, $x > 0$.

   Express $f(5)$ as a fraction with a rational denominator.   2

MARKS

DO NOT WRITE IN THIS MARGIN

10. Sketch the graph of $y = (x-3)^2 + 1$.

On your sketch, show clearly the coordinates of the turning point and the point of intersection with the y-axis.

3

MARKS | DO NOT WRITE IN THIS MARGIN

11. Simplify

$$\tan^2 x^\circ \cos^2 x^\circ \, .$$

Show your working.

2

[Turn over

MARKS

12. The diagrams below show a rectangle and a triangle.

All measurements are in centimetres.

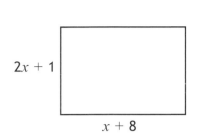
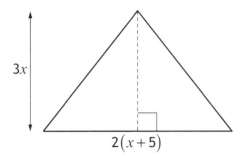

(a) Find an expression for the area of the **rectangle**.

1

(b) Given that the area of the rectangle is equal to the area of the triangle, show that $x^2 - 2x - 8 = 0$.

3

MARKS | DO NOT WRITE IN THIS MARGIN

12. (continued)

(c) Hence find, **algebraically**, the length and breadth of the rectangle.   3

[END OF QUESTION PAPER]

MARKS | DO NOT WRITE IN THIS MARGIN

ADDITIONAL SPACE FOR ANSWERS

Page fourteen

MARKS
DO NOT
WRITE IN
THIS
MARGIN

ADDITIONAL SPACE FOR ANSWERS

MARKS | DO NOT WRITE IN THIS MARGIN

ADDITIONAL SPACE FOR ANSWERS

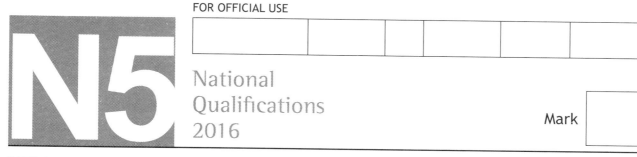

FOR OFFICIAL USE

N5

National Qualifications 2016

Mark

X747/75/02

Mathematics
Paper 2

THURSDAY, 12 MAY
2:20 PM — 3:50 PM

Total marks — 50

Attempt ALL questions.

You may use a calculator.

Full credit will be given only to solutions which contain appropriate working.

State the units for your answer where appropriate.

Write your answers clearly in the spaces provided in this booklet. Additional space for answers is provided at the end of this booklet. If you use this space you must clearly identify the question number you are attempting.

Use **blue** or **black** ink.

Before leaving the examination room you must give this booklet to the Invigilator; if you do not, you may lose all the marks for this paper.

FORMULAE LIST

The roots of $ax^2 + bx + c = 0$ are $x = \dfrac{-b \pm \sqrt{(b^2 - 4ac)}}{2a}$

Sine rule: $\dfrac{a}{\sin A} = \dfrac{b}{\sin B} = \dfrac{c}{\sin C}$

Cosine rule: $a^2 = b^2 + c^2 - 2bc\cos A$ or $\cos A = \dfrac{b^2 + c^2 - a^2}{2bc}$

Area of a triangle: $A = \frac{1}{2}ab\sin C$

Volume of a sphere: $V = \frac{4}{3}\pi r^3$

Volume of a cone: $V = \frac{1}{3}\pi r^2 h$

Volume of a pyramid: $V = \frac{1}{3}Ah$

Standard deviation: $s = \sqrt{\dfrac{\Sigma(x - \bar{x})^2}{n-1}}$

or $s = \sqrt{\dfrac{\Sigma x^2 - \dfrac{(\Sigma x)^2}{n}}{n-1}}$, where n is the sample size.

MARKS | DO NOT WRITE IN THIS MARGIN

Total marks — 50

Attempt ALL questions

1. A drinks manufacturer is reducing the sugar content of one of their fizzy drinks by 8% per year over the next 3 years.

   The sugar content of a standard can is currently 35 grams.

   Calculate the sugar content of a standard can after 3 years.   **3**

   $$35 \times 0.92^3 = 27.25$$

2. A pollen sample weighs 12 grams

   and contains 1.5×10^9 pollen grains.

   Calculate the weight of **one** pollen grain in grams.

   Give your answer in scientific notation.   **2**

   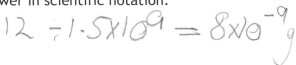

   $$12 \div 1.5 \times 10^9 = 8 \times 10^{-9} g$$

MARKS | DO NOT WRITE IN THIS MARGIN

3. The diagram below shows parallelogram ABCD.

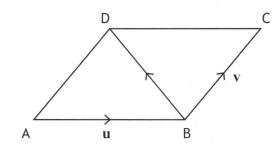

$\overrightarrow{AB}$ represents vector **u** and $\overrightarrow{BC}$ represents vector **v**.

Express $\overrightarrow{BD}$ in terms of **u** and **v**.   1

$-\vec{u}+\vec{v}$

$V-U$

4. Factorise fully $3x^2 - 48$.   2

$3x^2-48$

$3(x^2-16)$

$3x^2 - 48$

5. The diagram below shows a circle, centre O.

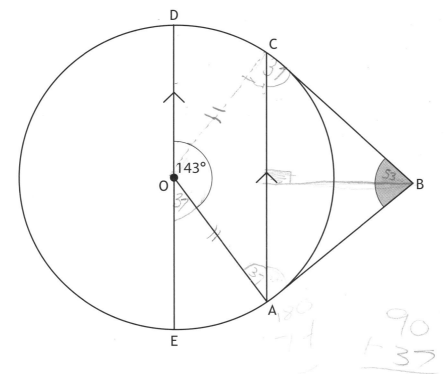

- AB and CB are tangents to the circle.
- AC and ED are parallel.
- Angle AOD is 143°.

Calculate the size of angle ABC.   3

[Turn over

MARKS

6. Jack called his internet provider on six occasions to report connection problems.

On each occasion he noted the length of time he had to wait before speaking to an adviser.

The times (in minutes) were as follows:

$$13 \quad 16 \quad 10 \quad 22 \quad 5 \quad 12$$

(a) Calculate the mean and standard deviation of these times. **4**

$$13+16+10+22+5+12 = 68$$

$$78 \div 6 = 13$$

		$\frac{x^2}{2}$
13	$-13 = 0$	0
16	$-13 = 3$	9
10	$-13 = -3$	9
22	$-13 = 9$	81
5	$-13 = -8$	64
12	$-13 = -1$	1
		174

$$\sqrt{\frac{171}{5}} = 5.848076607$$

$$= 5.85$$

MARKS | DO NOT WRITE IN THIS MARGIN

6. (continued)

(b) Sophie also called the same internet provider, on several occasions, to report connection problems.

Her mean waiting time was 15 minutes and the standard deviation was 4·3 minutes.

Make two valid comments comparing Sophie's waiting times with Jack's waiting times.

2

On Average Sophie had to wait longer than Jack

Sophies waiting time, on average, way more consistent

[Turn over

MARKS | DO NOT WRITE IN THIS MARGIN

7. A carton is in the shape of a large cone with a small cone removed.

The large cone has diameter of 32 cm and height 24 cm.

The small cone has diameter of 18 cm and height 13·5 cm.

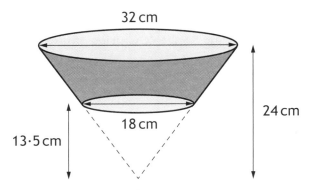

32 cm

24 cm

18 cm

13·5 cm

Calculate the volume of the carton.

Give your answer correct to 2 significant figures.

5

small cone $\frac{1}{3}\pi r^2 h$

$V = \frac{1}{3} \times \pi \times 9^2 \times 13\cdot5 = 11\cdot45\cdot11\,0522\,cm^3$

large cone Volume $= \frac{1}{3}\pi \times 18^2 \times 24$

$V = 6433\cdot981755$

$- 1145\cdot10522$

$5288\cdot871233\,cm^3$

MARKS | DO NOT WRITE IN THIS MARGIN

8. A set of stepladders has legs 150 centimetres and 140 centimetres long.

When the stepladder is fully open, the angle between the longer leg and the ground is 66°.

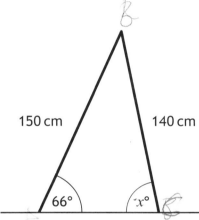

Calculate $x°$, the size of the angle between the shorter leg and the ground.   3

$$\frac{Sin A}{a} = \frac{Sin B}{b} = \frac{Sin C}{c}$$

$$\frac{Sin(66)}{140} = \frac{Sin B}{6} = \frac{x}{150}$$

$$\frac{Sin 66}{140} = \frac{x}{150}$$

$$\frac{Sin 66 \times 150}{140} = 0.978798706$$

$$Sin^{-1}(0.978...) = 78°$$

Page nine   [Turn over

9. Express $x^2 + 8x - 7$ in the form $(x+a)^2 + b$.

2

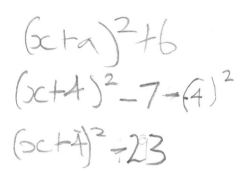

$$(x+a)^2 + b$$

$$(x+4)^2 - 7 - (4)^2$$

$$(x+4)^2 - 23$$

10. Simplify $\left(n^2\right)^3 \times n^{-10}$.

Give your answer with a **positive** power.

3

$$\left(n^2\right)^3 \times n^{-10}$$

$$n^6 \, x^{-10}$$

$$n^{-4}$$

$$\frac{1}{n^4}$$

MARKS | DO NOT WRITE IN THIS MARGIN

11. Two pictures are mathematically similar in shape.

100 cm

60 cm

The cost of each picture is proportional to its area.

The large picture costs £13·75.

Find the cost of the small picture.

3

$\div 100(00) = 13.75 \div 100$

$k_n = £0.1375$

$60 \times 0.1375 = £8.25$

MARKS

12. Change the subject of the formula $L = \sqrt{4kt - p}$ to k.   **3**

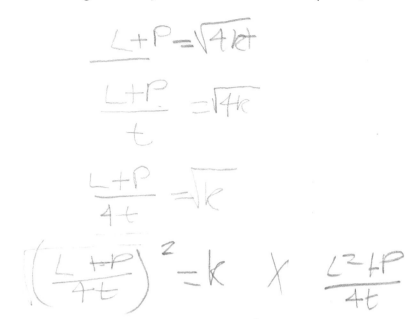

$$L + P = \sqrt{4kt}$$

$$\frac{L+P}{t} = \sqrt{4k}$$

$$\frac{L+P}{4t} = \sqrt{k}$$

$$\left(\frac{L+P}{4t}\right)^2 = k \qquad \times \qquad \frac{L^2 + P}{4t}$$

13. Express

$$\frac{3}{x-2} + \frac{5}{x+1}, \qquad x \neq 2, x \neq -1$$

as a single fraction in its simplest form.   **3**

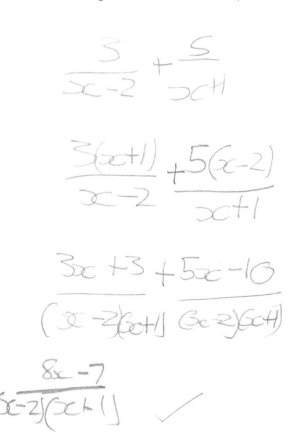

$$\frac{3}{x-2} + \frac{5}{x+1}$$

$$\frac{3(x+1)}{x-2} + \frac{5(x-2)}{x+1}$$

$$\frac{3x+3+5x-10}{(x-2)(x+1)\ (x-2)(x+1)}$$

$$\frac{8x-7}{(x-2)(x+1)} \qquad \checkmark$$

MARKS | DO NOT WRITE IN THIS MARGIN

14. Solve the equation $2 \tan x° + 5 = -4$, for $0 \le x \le 360$.

3

$2 \tan x + 5 = -4$

$2 \tan 4 + 5 = x$ x

$2 \tan 4 + 5 =$

[Turn over

MARKS | DO NOT WRITE IN THIS MARGIN

15. This perfume bottle has a label in the shape of part of a circle.

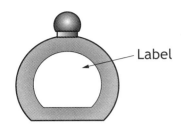

Label

A diagram of the label is shown below.

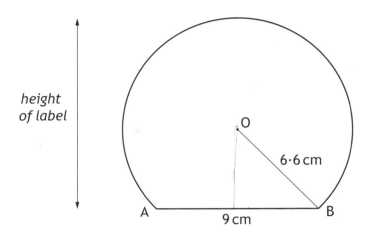

height
of label

O

6·6 cm

A   9 cm   B

- The centre of the circle is O.
- The chord AB is 9 centimetres.
- The radius OB is 6·6 centimetres.

Find the height of the label.   4

$6·6^2 + 9^2 = 23·31$

$\sqrt{23·31} = 4·828043082$

$= 4·8\,cm$

$\begin{array}{c} + 6·6 \\ \hline 11·4 \end{array}$

$h = 11·4\,cm^2$

MARKS | DO NOT WRITE IN THIS MARGIN

16. In the diagram below:

- DE is perpendicular to AC.
- AD = 4 centimetres.
- DB = 6 centimetres.
- AE = EC = 3 centimetres.

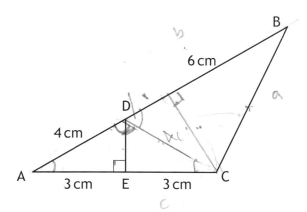

Calculate the length of BC.

Give your answer correct to one decimal place.   4

$$4^2 - 3^2 = \sqrt{7}$$
$$\sqrt{7} = 2.64575131 \, cm$$

$$\frac{Sin A}{a} = \frac{Sin B}{b}$$

$$Cos = c^2 + b^2 - 2 \times bc \, Cos$$

$$Cos \quad 10^2 + 6^2 - 2 \times 6 \times 10 \times Cos(41.4\ldots)$$

$$136 \quad - \quad 90$$

$$\frac{Sin(9B)}{4} = \frac{Sin x}{2.64575131}$$

$$a^2 = 46$$
$$a = \sqrt{46}$$
$$6.8$$

$$Sin x = 41.4096211$$

[END OF QUESTION PAPER]

MARKS DO NOT WRITE IN THIS MARGIN

ADDITIONAL SPACE FOR ANSWERS

MARKS

ADDITIONAL SPACE FOR ANSWERS

Page seventeen

MARKS | DO NOT WRITE IN THIS MARGIN

ADDITIONAL SPACE FOR ANSWERS

NATIONAL 5

Answers

SQA & HODDER GIBSON NATIONAL 5 MATHEMATICS 2016

NATIONAL 5 MATHEMATICS MODEL PAPER

Paper 1

1. $2\frac{5}{6}$

2. $6x^3 - x^2 + 13x - 10$

3. $m = (kL)^2$ **or** $m = k^2L^2$

4. (a) $2\mathbf{u} + \mathbf{v}$

   (b) $\mathbf{v} - \mathbf{u}$

5. $34°$

6. $\dfrac{3y}{y + 3}$

7. 27

8. (a) $x = 2$

   (b) 9

9. $(4, 5)$

10. $a = 5$, $b = 4$

11. $\cos B = \dfrac{3^2 + 6^2 - 5^2}{2 \times 3 \times 6} = \dfrac{20}{36} = \dfrac{5}{9}$

12. $6\sqrt{2}$

13. $\dfrac{7m + 3}{m(m + 1)}$

14. discriminant = 24; roots are real since discriminant > 0 and irrational since discriminant is not a perfect squrare.

Paper 2

1. £684·70

2. (a) mean = 7, standard deviation = 3·96

   (b) Under the new coach, the team scores more points and is more consistent.

3. M(0, 1, 0), N(4, 2, 2)

4. $y = 3x - 1$

5. arc AB = 0·88 metres; this is less than 0·9 metres, so the staircase will not pass the safety regulations.

6. 5400 cm^3

7. £860

8. 18·3 metres

9. 15 cm^2

10. 1503·5 cm^2

11. (a) -3

    (b) 11·5°, 168·5°

12. 0·35 metres

13. (a) $x^2 + 5 = 3(2x)$
    $$x^2 + 5 = 6x$$
    $$x^2 - 6x + 5 = 0$$

    (b) 5

NATIONAL 5 MATHEMATICS 2014

Paper 1

1. $\frac{25}{27}$

2. $6x^2 - 13x - 5$

3. $(x - 7)^2 - 5$

4. $\begin{bmatrix} -4 \\ 10 \\ 3 \end{bmatrix}$

5. 8 cm

6. (a) $C = 15F + 125$

   (b) 725 calories

7. $a = 5$

8. $9\sqrt{10}$

9. 600 000

10. $a = 3$, $b = -40$

11. (a) gradient $= -\frac{4}{3}$

    (b) (3,0)

12. 18 centimetres

13. (a) 6 seconds

    (b) No, because its maximum height is 64 metres

Paper 2

1. 590

2. B (8, 4, 10), C (4, 0, 10)

3. (a) $5a + 3c = 158 \cdot 25$

   (b) $3a + 2c = 98$

   (c) Adult ticket costs £22·50
       Child tickets costs £15·25

4. (a) (i) $\overline{x} = 56 \cdot 5$
       (ii) $s = 2 \cdot 4$

   (b) No, standard deviation is greater
       or
       No, times are more spread out

5. 3072 cm^3

6. No, with valid reason, eg as the triangle is not right angled since $110^2 \neq 75^2 + 85^2$

7. 150 cm^3

8. $5n^4$

9. $\dfrac{4x - 15}{x(x + 5)}$

10. (a) $84 \cdot 8°$

    (b) $155 \cdot 2°$

11. $a = \dfrac{2(s - ut)}{t^2}$

12. $x = 63°, 297°$

13. $151 \cdot 3$ m^2

NATIONAL 5 MATHEMATICS 2015

Paper 1

1. $3\frac{13}{15}$ or $\frac{58}{15}$

2. $x > -5$

3. $39°$

4. $x^3 - 3x^2 - 6x + 8$

5. $a = 8$

6. $a = 4, b = 3$

7. (a) (i) -2

    (ii) -4

   (b) $x = 2$

8. $y = 2x + 9$

9. $\cos100°$, $\cos90°$, $\cos300°$; with justification, e.g. $\cos100°$ is negative, $\cos90°$ is zero and $\cos300°$ is positive (or similar)

10. (a) median = 19·5, SIQR = 4·5

    (b) valid comments e.g.:

    • On average the second round's scores are higher

    • The second round's scores are more consistent

11. $x = 7, y = -2$

12. $\dfrac{x}{x + 5}$

13. $\sqrt{2}$

14. 32

Paper 2

1. £253 628 (·16)

2. $a = 7$

3. 0·78 km

4. 23

5. $\begin{bmatrix} -1 \\ -2 \end{bmatrix}$

6. (a) $1·1 \times 10^{12}$ km^3

   (b) 50 times bigger

7. $10s$

8. £350

9. 225 cm^2

10. 25 cm

11. 1039·2 cm^2

12. 1·99 m

13. 23·8 km

14. (a) (i) $2x + 13$

    (ii) $4x^2 + 44x + 117 = 270$

    $\Rightarrow 4x^2 + 44x - 153 = 0$

   (b) $x = 2·8$ cm

NATIONAL 5 MATHEMATICS 2016

Paper 1

1. $\begin{bmatrix} -3 \\ -4 \end{bmatrix}$

2. $\dfrac{13}{28}$

3. 157 cm^2

4. (a) $2c + 3d = 9\cdot6$

   (b) $3c + 4d = 13\cdot3$

   (c) A cloak requires 1·5 m^2 of material; a dress requires 2·2 m^2 of material

5. (a) $W = 20A + 40$

   (b) $20 \times 12 + 40 = 280$ kg

6. Real and distinct

7. (a) (8, 4, 0)

   (b) 7

8. $x = -\dfrac{5}{8}$

9. $\dfrac{2\sqrt{5}}{5}$

10.

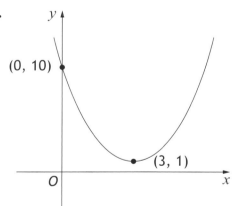

11. $\sin^2 x\,^\circ$

12. (a) $(2x + 1)(x + 8)$

    (b) $2x^2 + 16x + x + 8 = 3x^2 + 15x$

    $\Rightarrow x^2 - 2x - 8 = 0$

    (c) 12 cm and 9 cm

Paper 2

1. 27(·25408) grams

2. 8×10^{-9} grams

3. v − u

4. $3(x + 4)(x - 4)$

5. ABC = 74°

6. (a) Mean = 13 minutes, standard deviation = 5·7 minutes

   (b) Valid statements, eg, on average Sophie's waiting time was longer; Sophie's waiting times were more consistent

7. 5300 cm^3

8. 78°

9. $(x + 4)^2 - 23$

10. $\dfrac{1}{n^4}$

11. £4·95

12. $k = \dfrac{L^2 + p}{4t}$

13. $\dfrac{8x - 7}{(x - 2)(x + 1)}$

14. $x = 102\cdot5\,°, 282\cdot5\,°$

15. 11·4 … cm

16. 6·8 cm

Acknowledgements

Permission has been sought from all relevant copyright holders and Hodder Gibson is grateful for the use of the following:

Image © Anton Balazh/Shutterstock.com (2015 Paper 2 page 7);
Image © g215/Shutterstock.com (2016 Paper 2 page 3);
Image © Le Do/Shutterstock.com (2016 Paper 2 page 9);
Image © han871111/Shutterstock.com (2016 Paper 2 page 11).

Hodder Gibson would like to thank SQA for use of any past exam questions that may have been used in model papers, whether amended or in original form.